MORE
than a....
HIGH

MORE than a.... HIGH

moving from
spiritual high to
spiritual growth

CHARLIE ALCOCK

wph wesleyan
publishing
house

Indianapolis, Indiana

Copyright © 2007 by Charlie Alcock
Published by Wesleyan Publishing House
Indianapolis, Indiana 46250
Printed in the United States of America

ISBN: 978-0-89827-362-5

Library of Congress Cataloging-in-Publication Data

Alcock, Charlie.
  More than a high : moving from spiritual high to spiritual growth /
Charlie Alcock.
      p. cm.
  ISBN 978-0-89827-362-5
  1. Spiritual formation. I. Title.
  BV4511.A43 2007
  248.8'3--dc22
                                              2007014680

CONTENTS

To my mom. There will never be enough words to express how much I love and respect you. Your example and commitment to others is the greatest picture of Christ that I have ever known.

INTRODUCTION

It's over. The excitement you felt at the moment you gave your life to God has faded. The music is silent. The worship band has packed up their gear and is headed to the next gig. You're back in school, back in the cycle. You're wondering if what you experienced was even real. You wonder if God has stopped working in your life.

In these times, what you need most is not another hyped, emotional experience, but to be quiet and listen for what God is doing and wants to do in your life. What does He want to accomplish in you? If it is just going to be another year, another semester at school, then what's it all for? It

8

doesn't make sense that God just rewinds time and plays it over again. There's no way that God repeats the same old stuff. He wants to do something fresh and unique in you. He never stops working.

The danger is when we stop working, when we stop anticipating God's work. The secret to staying fresh in your relationship with Christ is found in this word: *anticipation*.

Always be expecting and wanting more.

Anticipate it.

Believe that He has more. He wants to do something fresh. Don't grow old and stale, thinking that you've experienced all that God has to offer. For most of you, you're just beginning your experience with Him—your life, your relationship.

It's now that you establish a pattern. It's now that you make the decision, "I'm in it all the way, and I will never, ever, ever settle for anything less. Never. I personally will not quit and get dry, crusty, and old in my relationship with Christ." You have to believe that He has a lot more in store for you. He's got a lot more than you've ever seen. Embrace Him.

The question, then, is are you willing to go to the next level? Are you willing to sacrifice to the point that you see Him move? For me, that means getting rid of a lot of Charlie to see more of God. I've seen enough of me, and it's not all that great. I bet, at this point in your life, you've seen enough of you. I have counseled many students through the years who looked in the mirror and couldn't stand what they saw. They didn't want to be who they were, and they hated seeing their reflection.

I want you to get to the point where you look in the mirror and see Christ's reflection.

It's time to make some changes and fight for your relationship with God. I'm talking about a spiritual tenacity that just doesn't quit.

Spiritual highs fade because they're based on emotions. Don't miss what I mean here. Emotions are not bad. They cause us to do things we wouldn't normally do. They cause us to fall in love, sing at the top of our lungs, and follow God. But relationships can't be built on emotions. Your experience with God is more than a series of spiritual highs. It's a relationship that bursts into being through emotion, but is sustained by passion, sweat-dripping

9

service, and unwavering faith. It's time for you to take the steps to becoming who God created you to be. It's time to change.

The following chapters will help you walk through the process of participating with God as He continues, and deepens, His work in you long after the moment of salvation. Please don't go through this book alone. You need the support of a group. The questions at the end of each chapter are designed to help you process in a group setting what you will read. It's important to write down your thoughts and answers in the space provided. Be honest and open as you share.

I pray God's blessing over you as you open your heart to the work He's doing in your life.

SOMETHING
to
BELIEVE
in

a few years ago, I was flying from San Diego, California, to Tulsa, Oklahoma, to start a youth camp. I was exhausted. I felt physically and spiritually spent. Now I've heard evangelists talk about mass revival on plane rides. You know, there were a thousand people on their flight, and the plane was about a half-mile long. Pretty soon they were talking to five people, and they had an altar call. The whole plane got saved, and the whole city they were flying over got saved. By the time they landed, the air traffic control people were crying and weeping. I knew I wasn't going to experience that this time.

I sat down on this particular flight, sandwiched between two people who obviously didn't understand the concept of personal space. I met them and, luckily, neither one was interested in a conversation. The plane took off, and it was bumpy and shaking for the first hour. All I wanted to do was get some sleep, but instead I started having a weird daydream. I felt like I was speaking to a large group of people and the message was intense. It was very awkward for me on the plane because I knew I started to cry. I tried to pretend like I was sleeping, but I felt such an intense conviction. I got a piece of paper and started writing as fast as I could. What follows is that message.

a creed for this generation

This generation, your generation, has grown up in an age of deception and lies. You have seen spiritual leaders fail morally and political leaders lie openly. You have been raised in an age of mass media to the point that the lines of entertainment and reality are indistinguishable, and even worse, one and the same. What is seen from ABC to MTV has become, in effect, your window to the world, one that is void of absolutes and morals. Truths once learned in Sunday school are seen as rigid and old-fashioned instead of fundamental and important. This generation mocks a biblical view of freedom, arguing that it strangles individuality. Christians are depicted as stiff, mindless people, closed off to anything new or innovative. Principles that the Church stands on are constantly slurred into positions of intolerance and prejudice.

The core of this generation has crumbled in this age of deception and lies. History will remember it as one of great individualism and creativity. But we have clearly lost our way. The truth is that there is a pressure to go and to do even if we don't know why, when, or where. When it comes to your relationship with God, you are generally tired, spent, and unable to dive in. And here's the killer: when you're unable to dive in spiritually, you feel guilty. Guilt prevents you from accepting God's grace and His love. I don't think another generation has had to deal with the amount of guilt you do because of what you are exposed to every day. It's so easy to fall. You know it. I know it. I don't need to give you any illustrations. It's intense. And guilt is a major tool that Satan uses to keep you from becoming passionate in your relationship with Christ.

Everything you see and hear in the media or elsewhere is a call for independence. There is no real understanding

13

of fundamental truth. Independence for the sake of independence is the resounding chorus. This cultural cry for freedom provides the opportunity, but it doesn't care about your safety. You are jumping out of an airplane without a parachute. The world doesn't care what happens to you when you fall to your death. In fact, you are forgotten the moment you jump. The world is only concerned with the thrill and satisfaction of jumping—and the promise, the energy, the good time, the party that comes with it.

Without Christ there is no purpose. It's easy to experience God fully and then go back to school and act the same as everybody else.

Trusting in Him, relying on His strength, has to become the cause you fight for.

To be like Christ is the challenge. He is the one who gives you distinction, identity, purpose, and place. And above all else, He is the only one who gives you everlasting life, something this world cannot compete with. It doesn't have it. It doesn't understand it—the call to be authentic, to be real, to be free, not in our ability to create or to manipulate, but in complete faith, believing that only through total abandonment will He produce in you the life you seek. You must let Him have control. Trust in Him with what you want, with what you have, and with what you hope to be. He will develop you into the person He created you to be.

Your responsibility is to stay focused on Christ. You have the only thing culture cannot recreate. So sing it, pray it, believe it, stand on it, and be lost in it. For in being lost you are humbled to the point of full surrender. It is at that point that you are truly found. How crazy is that? You are truly found when you are lost in Christ. You know what freedom is? Freedom is full surrender. You know what the biggest sin was? It was Satan wanting to be like God. All sin is connected to selfishness. And all freedom is connected to self*less*ness.

We think freedom is doing it our way. True freedom is being able to walk out into the world, knowing that regardless of what happens you are connected to Almighty God. True freedom is knowing that the temptations you face no longer have any power over you.

> You, however, are not controlled by the sinful nature but are in the Spirit, if indeed the Spirit of God lives in you. And if anyone does not have

> the Spirit of Christ, they do not belong to Christ. But if Christ is in you, then even though your body is subject to death because of sin, the Spirit gives life because of righteousness. (Rom. 8:9–10)

Are you experiencing true freedom?

It's time for Christians to be countercultural. We've become a selfish generation that sees everything based on our own wants and desires. For way too long I've been at the front of that pack, and it doesn't produce anything—except failure. And after tons of failure, people you know—and maybe even you yourself—will walk away from Christ. Dying to self, dying to desire, dying to hopes, dying to dreams. What's it going to cost you to stay passionate? You need to get to the point where you're not afraid to be exposed. You're not afraid to say, "Listen, I'm wrong here, and I've failed here." It's hard to be exposed. I've been in accountability with a group of my friends for years, and it's tough. It's very, very difficult to say when you're wrong. But it's liberating. After you've walked through that time of fear, and you deal with the situation, there's a peace and an authenticity—it's liberating. It's freedom. I want you to know freedom.

But listen, there is a cost. You might have to throw some stuff away. You might have to say no to stuff you really want to do. You might have to redefine your relationship with your girlfriend or your boyfriend. There might be a lot of stuff that you have to do that might cost you friends. I don't know. But if you want to know freedom, it's a small price to pay. So let's take a journey; let's keep moving forward. God is not finished. Let's be a part of something that's bigger than we are.

17

Discussion Questions

Remember, these questions are designed to help you (and your discipleship group) process what you have just read. It's important to write down your response in the space provided.

1. How has culture influenced you?

2. What do people at your school say about Christians?

3. Are most people okay with your being a Christian, or do they judge you more than others?

4. What do you value most in your life? (You can answer this question best by looking at how you spend your time.)

5. How can you make more time to focus on your relationship with God?

19

6. What is true freedom?

7. List some things that you will have to sacrifice to follow God.

BEYOND
the
MOMENT

In the first chapter we looked at the effect of culture on your spiritual walk. It is my desire, now, to help you understand your emotionally charged experiences of God so that they will go beyond the moment. I can't stand going to events when they're too focused on the moment. Moments are temporary and lack any lasting effect—unless they grow up and become movements. But do you know why the moments are so good at these events? The spirit of expectancy. You go and expect God to move. You expect intense worship. You expect God to speak to you. The big problem is that when the moment passes, you don't expect as much from God. When you go to your youth group, do you expect God to move? Do you expect Him to do something? Do you expect to engage and raise your hands in worship? Most don't.

Most of the time we're at our home churches, and it's different. The music is different. The speaking is different. But what you experience is not driven by a style or a location. It's driven by a Person. You've got to embrace this understanding as we go deeper. You can choose to grow and mature spiritually in any setting, regardless of style. And you can't wait for anyone else to push you into it. You can't wait for something to happen that just blows you away. You have to engage, not with what is said or sung from stage, but with what God has written and said. It doesn't matter how good the speaker is, and it doesn't matter how good the music is because you can grab anything at any point, at any time.

I would always go to my home church after a big event, and the pastor would ask the youth group about our experience. We would speak in front of the church and give our testimonies. That's where the high would end for me. The thing is, I was the barrier. I'm the one who shut down my intense connection with God.

I tell you right now, your home church is not the sole vehicle that drives your spirituality. It is a precious vehicle but not the only one. And it definitely isn't a barrier to spiritual growth. It is your responsibility to grow in your relationship with Christ. A lot of people have told me, though, that it's the local church that has caused them not to grow, but I say that that's sick and cannot be true. Your church cannot keep you from growing; you keep you from growing. They say, "But the music just isn't my style, and when the guy preaches, I don't like it." That's immaturity. You've got to grow out of that mind-set. To continue to spiritually grow, you have to be able to embrace what God is saying through whatever means—whatever vehicle.

getting off the milk diet

What God desires for you cannot be realized in a moment. His desires can be identified, but they are realized in your life by living them out. That's the point of Christian events: to identify (1) who God says He is; (2) who you say He is; (3) His principles for life; (4) His desires for your life; and finally (5) how you will choose to live out what God wants. The real work doesn't begin at the event; it begins when you leave.

23

In this chapter I'm going to identify what that work is, and what the outcome should be. I'm tired of seeing us lose because we fail to identify up front what the goal line is. Can you imagine two football teams playing on a field with no goal lines? That doesn't make sense. Part of being a Christian is identifying the goal line so you know where you're going. As a young Christian I was stupid. I knew Jesus, but I didn't know what He wanted to do in my life or what He wanted me to do in response. We talk about who He is, and that's good, but if we don't talk about what He does, we fail.

> We have much to say about this, but it is hard to make it clear to you because you no longer try to understand. In fact, though by this time you ought to be teachers, you need someone to teach you the elementary truths of God's word all over again. You need milk, not solid food! Anyone who lives on milk, being still an infant, is not acquainted with the teaching about righteousness. But solid food is for the mature, who by constant use have trained themselves to distinguish good from evil. (Heb. 5:11–14)

Where are you at in your Christian life? Are you still on milk? You get high off the worship experience, but when no one's around, it's really not happening. That's very elementary if you get a spiritual high only from the moment and that's it. If this is you, and if you're tired of milk and want to dive deeper into who God is, this is what I want you to do:

1. *Reject the pull to mediocrity.* Mediocrity is to just sit and be spoon-fed. You reject this pull when you intentionally run after God each day.

2. *See if something is pleasing to God before you commit to it yourself.* When you take this step, so much of your life will be cleaned up. The music you listen to, the movies you watch, the things you do with your friends when you are just hanging out—are they pleasing to God? Here's an easy test. When you are in tune with God, you'll have conviction. Conviction is healthy. It's good. It's something God gives you to help you keep on track. It's that whispering voice inside you that says "don't!" Don't see it as an irritation; see it as a blessing. What I'm concerned about is this: the little things in your life that you allow to infiltrate your mind and your thinking. You let yourself slide a little bit, and a little bit more, and a little bit more—to the

25

point that you're way off course. But conviction will help to keep you walking in a straight line.

3. *Read the Bible every day.* To know what's pleasing to God you have to get into His Word. Christian events are such intense spiritual experiences because you are constantly diving into God's Word. You hear it and read it multiple times a day, but when you go home, the Bible goes back under your bed, and things fall apart. This point is a continual decision you will have to make. A good friend of mine always poses this question to me: "Are you going to choose the pain of discipline or the pain of regret?"

4. *Learn how to listen to His voice.* We live in a time and an age where listening is not that big of a deal. This is arrogance not maturity. If you want to be proactive as a Christian, if you want to be a biblical Christian, then you've got to hear God's voice, and you can't when you are constantly distracted. And you know how that is. You are listening to so much other stuff that you simply can't hear God. In fact, you learn to tune Him out. We're so good at that as Christians. But there is nothing more important in your life than God's voice. You've got to know when He's calling you. You've got to know when He's saying something to you. In fact, you've got

to learn how to get rid of all of the distractions in your life and focus in on God's voice. If you don't hear Him speaking to you, then something is wrong. Learn to ask yourself, "What am I surrounded by that is preventing me from hearing God's voice?"

I've got to hear God speaking to me, because if I don't, I'm lost. I don't have direction. I need my God because He is the one who created me. He's the one who loves me. He's the one who tests me, and without Him, I am nothing.

Reject mediocrity. Do what pleases God. Read the Bible. Know His voice. The message is simple, but the process is so, so hard. The battle begins when you leave the moment. Where are you going to be when the spiritual high fades? How far down the road will you go? What would happen if you committed to hear His voice, to know it, and to listen for it? Imagine what it would be like. The more you hear Him, the more you will know Him, and the more you know Him, the more you will want to please Him.

Discussion Questions

Remember, these questions are designed to help you (and your discipleship group) process what you have just read. It's important to write down your response in the space provided.

1. What did it feel like to wait for Christmas morning as a kid?

2. Have you ever felt the same when thinking about spending time with God? Was it a camp, a concert, an event at church, or just being alone with God that excited you?

3. Do you feel you've grown spiritually this past year?

4. If you haven't, what do you think has kept you from growing spiritually?

5. What do you think God cares about?

6. Have you read the Bible lately?

30

7. What does God's voice sound like? How do you know when He speaks to you?

the
ROLLERCOASTER

growing up in Michigan I loved going on the youth group trip to Cedar Point (the greatest rollercoaster park in the world). It was there that I walked the long, lonely trail that led to Gemini. Yes, I was scared, but there were girls around so I acted tough. Gemini was a racing coaster, and only the committed waited in the extra long line to get the front seat, the seat of honor. The front seat, as you know, is only for those who have no fear. As I waited in that line my confidence grew. Train after train came back and everyone was still alive. A few of the riders looked like they had gotten sick, but I had a plan for that. If I was going to lose it (you know, vomit), then I would turn my head away from my friends. That's also another reason for sitting in the front! I braved Gemini that day, and from then on I was a fan of rollercoasters. No matter where we went, I couldn't wait to get off the bus and run to get a good place in line.

If there's one sermon I remember most from growing up, it has to be the sermon about the spiritual rollercoaster. I know I heard it at youth group, at camp, and at several retreats. I remember so clearly the old man who would howl those wretched words: "Quit riding the spiritual rollercoaster! Up and down, up and down. It's time to get off that thing." Regardless of how many times I heard that sermon, I just couldn't do it. I had a special reservation in the front car of that monster. Believe me; I tried to get off that thing a million times. I worked, I committed, I prayed, and I cried, but to no avail. Yes, I knew God had saved me. Yes, I knew God loved me. Yes, I wanted so badly to keep from being a hypocrite and not run hot and cold. Still I constantly fought the nasty rollercoaster syndrome—up and down, up and down. All through high school I was haunted by the rollercoaster syndrome, and things didn't change until I went to college.

your emotional tide

One day in a general psychology class I heard something that was so simple, yet deeply profound. I remember hearing the professor talk in class about emotions. She talked to us about our emotional makeup and how we all have an emotional tide. Just like the waves in the ocean come in and go out with the tide, we as human beings have an emotional tide. There are days that our emotional tide is out (down) and we don't feel that great. Regardless of how good the day is or how things have been going for us that week, we just don't wake up feeling ready to take on the world. When our emotional tide is in (up), we could be facing some very hard times, but we wake up ready to take life on.

Your emotional tide is an intrinsic (inside you) factor. There are forces from the outside that can influence your emotional tide, though. These factors could be linked to circumstances that are driven by things that happen around you: someone says something mean to you, a bad grade on a test, an accident. All these things are extrinsic (outside you) factors. That professor taught me two very important lessons. First, understand that you have an emotional tide. Second, don't connect your spiritual life

33

to your emotional tide. If you do, you will always be inconsistent.

34

Fast forward seven years from college, and I was a youth pastor at camp with my own youth group. It was a great week and we all were on a spiritual high. I remember the whole youth group sitting around after the evening rally, talking about what God had done in our lives. Then Staci spoke up. She asked a question that sounded so familiar to me.

"How can we make this spiritual high our spiritual norm?"

Wow! Staci not only posed that question to us at camp, but a few days later on Sunday morning she stood up and asked that question to the entire church. You don't know Staci, but the question remains. How can you make the spiritual highs you experience turn into your spiritual norm? How can you jump off the spiritual rollercoaster?

Let's go back to the profound message of my college professor. We don't have to allow our emotional tide to dictate how we live spiritually. That's what I used to do. I could not separate my emotional tide (how I felt) from my spiritual life (what I knew to be true). I allowed circumstances, both within my control and outside it, to rob me of my spiritual integrity. The spiritual rollercoaster thrives on your not knowing the difference between your emotional tide and your spiritual life. I know you don't desire to run hot and cold as a Christian. I know you haven't made a commitment to God, only to simply forget about it and then move on. I think you, like me, really want the commitments you've made to last for a lifetime. I believe you, like me (and like Staci), want to make the spiritual high you've felt your spiritual norm.

So start. Start by understanding that what you felt in the spiritually intense moment was not just the emotion, it was based on fact. Recognize the difference between your emotional tide and your spiritual life. Yes, when your emotional tide is high, you will feel more spiritual. And when your emotional tide is low, you will feel less spiritual. But your spiritual reality is not connected to how you feel. Your spiritual reality is that God continues His work deep within your soul regardless of how you feel.

Your identity in Christ doesn't change with your emotions.

35

I want you to go back and remember when you asked Christ into your life. I want you to understand that a massive change took place deep within your soul. Before Christ came into your life, you were still a person created in God's image. Before you asked Christ to take over your life, you were a person that God created with a unique personality and a style all your own. You had emotions and feelings. You had good days and bad days—and all of this before you asked Christ into your life. So what changed? Your heart changed. Your spirit changed. You went from being a sinner to a person who by grace is now a saint, a personal friend of Jesus. This produced a huge spiritual high. The problem came, though, a few days or weeks after the initial high.

You are a new creation, but that's not the end, only the beginning. So many people ask Christ into their life and then think they can go back to doing whatever they had been doing. Some think they won't struggle with the same things that they were struggling with before. Others think that all of the negative outside factors in their life will change, and they will not have to deal with any of those problems again. The truth is that asking Christ into your life changed your eternal destiny, but you must still live life on this earth with the same range of feelings and emotions you were born with. Asking Christ into your life is the first step. Growing in Christ and being consistent in your commitment to Christ, regardless of your emotional tide, are steps you will take every day for the rest of your life.

The rollercoaster stops here.

No longer is your relationship with Christ dictated by how you feel. After the emotional explosion of giving your life to Christ, your high will fade, but as you grow in Christ, your confidence in Christ will grow too. As you continually commit to Christ, your identity will develop in Him. You will live a consistent life, one that is committed to following God regardless of the tide. No question, this is way easier said than done, but you can have security in Christ that can't be lost by the moving of the emotional tide in your life. You can finally get off the ride.

Discussion Questions

Remember, these questions are designed to help you (and your discipleship group) process what you have just read. It's important to write down your response in the space provided.

1. Talk in your group about the times in your life when you felt separated from God.

2. Have you ever felt like you let God down?

3. When times are good, and you are on fire for God, list the reasons why you feel this way.

4. When times are bad, and you feel distant from God, list the reasons why you feel this way.

THE ROLLERCOASTER

5. What do you notice in other people when they are distant from God but used to be so close to Him?

40

6. How big a role do emotions play in your life? In your spiritual life?

7. How does hearing that your relationship with God is not based on how you feel change things for you?

MORE
than a
SERVANT

In this chapter we are going to study probably the single most life-changing passage of Scripture that I have ever read. I encourage you to engage this text with all your heart and mind, committing these words of Jesus to memory if you feel led.

> I am the true vine, and my Father is the gardener. He cuts off every branch in me that bears no fruit, while every branch that does bear fruit he prunes so that it will be even more fruitful. You are already clean because of the word I have spoken to you. Remain in me, as I also remain in you. No branch can

bear fruit by itself; it must remain in the vine. Neither can you bear fruit unless you remain in me.

I am the vine; you are the branches. If you remain in me and I in you, you will bear much fruit; apart from me you can do nothing. If you do not remain in me, you are like a branch that is thrown away and withers; such branches are picked up, thrown into the fire and burned. If you remain in me and my words remain in you, ask whatever you wish, and it will be done for you. . . .

I no longer call you servants, because servants do not know their master's business. Instead, I have called you friends, for everything that I learned from my Father I have made known to you. (John 15:1–7, 15)

the promise

I love that last verse. We are more than servants of God, though we do and should serve Him. We are His friends. Right now I simply want to walk you through this passage and give you a few key points to solidify what verse 15 makes very clear. Jesus began by explaining His relationship with the Father: "I am the true vine, and my Father is the gardener. He cuts off every branch in me that bears no fruit, while every branch that does bear fruit he prunes so that it will be even more fruitful" (verses 1–2). Pruning is an interesting trick of the gardener. It goes against logic. The gardener cuts away part of a healthy branch so that it will produce even more fruit. The Master Gardener will cut away at you even when you are healthy, to make you better. He will cut distractions out of your life. He will slice away bad attitudes and bad habits—if you let Him.

Don't resist this work, even when it hurts.

Jesus went on to define our relationship with Him. "I am the vine; you are the branches," He said. "If you remain in me and I in you, you will bear much fruit; apart from me you can do nothing" (verse 5). You *will* bear fruit. It's not a question. You *will* bear fruit. It's clear. It's a promise. It does not say, you might bear fruit, maybe, if you have the right style or if you have the right talents. If you can play the drums, the guitar, or if you're a good speaker or singer, then you will bear fruit. It doesn't say that at all. It's a promise to anyone and to everyone that if you remain in Him, you *will* bear fruit. And

43

44

do you know what kind of fruit He is talking about? The fruit of the Spirit—love, joy, peace, patience, kindness, goodness, faithfulness, gentleness, and self-control (Gal. 5:22–23).

Here's the best part: As you bear fruit, you move from being a servant to being a friend, a friend of Almighty God. I want you to tuck this promise deep inside your heart and mind. This promise does not depend on the gifts you have or who your mom and dad are or what your home or school situation is like. It's not dependent on anything like that. It only relies on this basic biblical principle: "If you remain in me." You can do that. You can remain in Him. The fruit is His. That's the good news. Your core responsibility is to remain in Jesus, the Vine. And He, then, produces fruit in you. And when people taste that fruit, they will know whose it is. Anything that I produce or that you produce, they will spit out of their mouth. But anything that comes from Almighty God is sweet. It's pure and innocent.

a cumulative effect

You probably carry with you memories of intense times at the altars of past spiritual experiences, of great times at camps or retreats, and of lessons learned at those events.

You probably also carry with you memories of failing year after year when you get back to school. Don't let experiences after big events—times you make mistakes and fall back into your old traps—wipe away all the good you learned and the commitments you made. That's not how it works. The experiences of your relationship with Jesus Christ are cumulative—they add on to each other, over and over and over. They grow. They're not wiped out. Do not listen to the enemy when he tries to nullify what Christ has done in you. He is a liar. You are connected to Almighty God. You are a friend of Christ. And the good you learn each year just builds on itself. The commitments you make are like stairs leading up to Christlikeness.

Therefore you can live in victory, not in fear of defeat. You can live in a relationship with Christ and not fear what Satan is going to do. You can have hope and not wonder when you will fail. No matter what happens to you or around you, the promise of God remains. That's freedom. That's freedom in Christ. And that's what you have when you remain in the Vine.

But failure is a tough mountain to climb, especially when your emotional tide recedes with the failure. A typical commitment made is trying to read through the whole

45

46

Bible in the next year. You start at Genesis, and it gets tough in a hurry, but you stick with it because you want to fulfill your commitment. When you fail, you feel even worse than when you started.

I want to give you a little encouragement with this cumulative effect I'm talking about. When you read through Scripture, it doesn't always make sense or give you warm, fuzzy feelings. Sometimes it's as dry as dust, but the core principle is this: As you read, what you're reading is stored in this complex, incredible thing called your brain.

And when it goes into your brain, it will come out in your life. God's Word never returns void. That means that no matter if you "feel" it working, it is working. As you're reading, you may not feel inspired all the time, but then all of the sudden, on week three of your reading through the Bible, it's like, "Wow, God! That makes so much sense." Boom. You start growing and growing and growing. It all adds up and bears fruit.

Jesus has given you a promise. "If you remain in me and I in you, you *will* bear much fruit." It's so sweet. It's so good. It's the best life possible. And it is possible. You are God's friend. Your failures do not wipe away your hunger and thirst for more of God. And as you are diligent in your study of Scripture and intimate in your worship, you will grow. You are growing. Now God is going to take you to the best part of this experience: He's going to let you shine His light in the world.

47

Discussion Questions

Remember, these questions are designed to help you (and your discipleship group) process what you have just read. It's important to write down your response in the space provided.

1. Why does a gardener prune a healthy plant?

2. What are some things you think God is pruning from your life?

3. How do you treat your friends when they let you down?

4. As friends of God, how does He treat us when we let Him down?

5. Do you feel like God's friend?

49

6. What is the cumulative effect of our relationship with God?

7. How can you help each other after one of you has failed God?

8. Write verse 15 in the space below and memorize it.

BECOMING
like
CHRIST

I understand that becoming like Christ sounds impossible. And on your own, it is impossible. But when you remain in Christ, He works in your life and in your heart to change you. He doesn't begin this work in you so that you spend the rest of your life chasing after an uncatchable dream. He molds and shapes your soul to reflect His life. He does this in reality. He takes your anger, your pride, and your lust and turns them into His love, humility, and self-control. This is why you give your life to Him—to be different.

The problem is that you give your life to Him and then take it right back. And I'm not just talking about falling back into the same old sins. You even take back your life to do what you think is best. You're hyped because of the experience at camp or retreat or whatever, and you get home and try to change yourself. You try to do the work of becoming like Christ on your own. I'm not saying that once you get home you have no work to do. You will participate with Christ as He changes you, but many times we try to go it alone. Going it alone only results in one thing: guilt. You can't change yourself. You fall back into the same old things you were doing before. And you feel guilty. In fact, you are overwhelmed by guilt, paralyzed by it. You give up and chalk up your experience with Christ as just emotion, and you wait for the next high.

I believe that a vast majority of students in this country fail to receive Christ, fail to want Christ, fail to stay connected to Christ because of an intense amount of guilt. This culture has seen more and knows more than any other that's ever existed on the planet. The Internet dominates. What's on TV dominates like never before. And we're way, way, way too experienced way, way, way too young. You know what I'm talking about. We talked about it in the very first chapter of this book.

This guilt will always strangle your spiritual life.

Satan knows this and loves to throw it in your face. He arouses this guilt in your heart and stokes it until it's red hot. He hits you from all directions after you have an explosive encounter with God. He knows your weaknesses and strategically places temptations in front of you that exploit those weaknesses. Then he lays on the guilt. Christ has come to set you free from guilt. Grace is not a license to do whatever you want, but it is your get-out-of-jail-free card when it comes to guilt.

stacking up the chairs

Picture a row of chairs, the stackable kind like you have at your church or school. Each chair represents a moment you have experienced God in a truly powerful way. One chair might represent when you gave your life to Christ as a young child. The next one might represent an experience at camp. In fact, a good number of them might represent different years of camps, retreats, or convention experiences. By the time you finish high school, you could have a large row of chairs.

Now I want you to stack the chairs. Remember that your relationship with God and your experiences of God have a cumulative effect. They build on each other. So stack these

53

54

moments with God. After you have stacked up two or three it looks pretty nice. Once you reach five or six chairs you start to get impressed. As the stack of chairs rises you feel pretty good about yourself, but remember that these are just moments with God. Your stack, no matter how impressive, is just a monument to those experiences. They have to become more than just moments we worship. They have to turn into movement. That's why this chapter is so important.

> **The intense times you have had with God are not meant to just be experienced by you. They are meant to change you.**

I'm not trying to downplay the experiences you've had with God. Those times were good and serve as reminders and motivators of the change you desperately desire. Those moments kick-started your relationship with God. Remember them. Cherish them. But don't get stuck with them. You have to keep moving. Paul said it best in his letter to the Colossians: "So then, just as you received Christ Jesus as Lord, continue to live your lives in him, rooted and built up in him, strengthened in the faith as you were taught, and overflowing with thankfulness" (Col. 2:6–7).

the process of becoming

What I want to do next is to give you some very practical ways that you can participate with Christ in the process of becoming like Him. It's lazy to think that all you have to do is just sit back and watch Christ work. He has invited you, as a friend, to work with Him. I'm not talking about work that leads to guilt or that earns your salvation for you. I'm talking about things that you can do that will open your heart more deeply to the work Christ is doing in you.

1. *Study the life of Jesus.* There's no better place to start than with the life of Jesus. You say you want to be like Christ. You sing about it. You pray about it. But do you really know how Jesus lived when He was on this earth? Sure you remember a few stories from when you were a kid, but do you really know how Jesus treated the people He hung out with? You will never really understand Christlikeness until you know who Christ is. The simple way to do this is to pick one of the Gospels (the first four books of the New Testament). Pick any Gospel—Matthew, Mark, Luke, or John. Pick one and read it. And I mean read it. Read it over and over again until you feel like you've got it. This could take weeks or months. If you start

to get bored with it, do more than just read it. Find creative ways to experience the passage. Buy an audio version of it and listen to it before you go to bed. Write a summary of the life of Jesus in your own words. Do whatever it takes to really absorb His life.

2. *Practice the disciplines Jesus modeled.* You'll notice from reading about Jesus' life that He did several things each day that helped keep His focus on God the Father. We call those things spiritual practices or disciplines. Don't get scared by the word *discipline*. It won't hurt as much as you think, but disciplines do require some effort on your part. Jesus often went out alone to pray. He also prayed with His disciples and studied the Scriptures with them. Jesus also fasted. This discipline should be practiced with wisdom, the right motive, and guidance from an older Christian. Don't skip lunch so that you'll fit into your bathing suit during the summer. Skip lunch every once in a while so that you can spend that time with God. These are just a few of the disciplines Jesus modeled. As you study His life, see how many more you find.

3. *Open your true heart to Him.* So many of us try to hide who we really are. You hide it from your friends, from your parents and teachers, but you know you can't hide it

from God. Intentionally open your heart to God each day, and invite Him to continue His work in your life. Give Jesus control of every area of your life. He knows your deepest thoughts, and He loves you completely. Stop hiding from His love.

57

Discussion Questions

Remember, these questions are designed to help you (and your discipleship group) process what you have just read. It's important to write down your response in the space provided.

1. What does it mean to be like Christ?

2. Do you find yourself falling into the same temptations once you get back home from an intense experience with God?

3. What does your stack of chairs look like?

4. What are some creative ways that you and your friends can study the life of Jesus?

5. What is a spiritual practice or discipline Jesus modeled?

60

6. When was the last time you went off by yourself to pray?

7. Why do you think it's a natural reaction to hide from God?

the AROMA of CHRIST

i love certain smells—the smell of a new car or a pair of new shoes. I love the smell of popcorn and the smell of fresh-cut grass, as weird as that sounds. But I love the smell of *carne asada* being cooked on a grill the best of all. Okay, maybe you have no clue what *carne asada* is, so let me explain. When I was a youth pastor in San Diego, I was going to meet with a student named Brandon for his lunch break from school. He insisted on meeting at a little Mexican dive called Las Parrillas. This was the sacred spot where Brandon introduced me to *carne asada*, a special marinated steak.

He ordered a *carne asada* quesadilla for me with a healthy side of fresh salsa and guacamole. After one bite I began to weep with joy as this incredible taste exploded in my mouth. That's a little over the top, but it was good, very good. I was hooked, and in San Diego there's no lack of good Mexican food. In fact, restaurants there compete as to who makes the best *carne asada*. This is great if you live in San Diego, but recently I moved back to Indiana, and no one here even knows how to pronounce the words. And let me be straight with you: fast food is not real Mexican food!

In a moment of grief and sorrow one day, I called my friend Bob in San Diego, hoping to maybe smell some *carne* cooking over the phone. Bob is an expert in so many things, but his secret to making *carne asada* has to be his greatest gift. On the phone that day, he could hear my desperation, so he revealed to me his secret marinade. I needed an onion, a few whole oranges, garlic powder, and salt. He told me to layer the meat with slices of the onion and oranges in a bowl, sprinkling in some garlic powder and salt. But here's the key: squeeze fresh orange juice between each layer. Then let it marinate.

I did it, but seriously, it smelled horrible. I hate the smell of onions. I didn't see how an onion would mix with oranges and garlic to make a good-tasting anything. After about twenty-four hours of the meat marinating, I didn't think I could eat what was in the bowl. I stayed faithful, however, and heated up the grill. I opened the lid of the grill and held my breath as I pulled out the slices of meat—then it happened. The moment the meat hit the grill, this incredible aroma poured out. Sweet! I ran and got my Mountain Dew, tortillas, salsa, and guacamole and went to town.

I get it now. The ingredients Bob gave me seemed insignificant and unrelated apart from each other. But once joined together, they work together to tenderize the meat and pack it full of flavor. The acids in the orange juice activate the other ingredients. The orange slices and onion break down and penetrate into the meat, allowing the garlic and salt to do their work. This process takes time. You have to be patient. If you try to grill the meat before it's time, you won't get that incredible flavor.

Then you add the fire, because until the meat is placed on the fire it can't release its incredible aroma. This aroma is

63

a signal to me and everybody within smelling distance that there is something really good to eat at my house.

You know where I'm going with this illustration. If you're going to be what God is calling you to be, you must understand this marinating process. I, like you, want to enjoy the end result, that incredible-tasting *carne asada* right off the grill, without taking the time to prepare it properly. Sure, you can pull up to a fast food place and get what you want in a matter of seconds, but what I'm talking about is worth the wait (and it's actually food).

You're smart; you can make the connections here. You must allow the Holy Spirit and the disciplines that Jesus modeled to work together in your life to transform you. Don't just embrace the ingredients you like, but rather, embrace all of them, knowing that they work together. We talked about these disciplines in the previous chapter: prayer, Bible study, accountability, worship, fasting. This process will also include times of tears and correction—the onions of the marinade. If you fail to recognize and engage all of these elements, you will fail to produce the aroma of Christ when you are tested by fire. All of us are being tested by fire, even now, and I want to ask you,

"What do you smell like to the rest of the world?"

> But thanks be to God, who always leads us as captives in Christ's triumphal procession and uses us to spread the aroma of the knowledge of him everywhere. For we are to God the pleasing aroma of Christ among those who are being saved and those who are perishing. (2 Cor. 2:14–15)

I believe it's your desire to honor Jesus in the way you live your life. The commitments you've made are part of the marinating process, but you must allow Him to complete His process in you. You have to submit to the process. You must allow yourself to marinate in Christ.

created for others

Let's go even deeper with this. When I think about how our lives have an aroma, it helps me to understand that our lives are meant to have an impact on other people. Yes, we are to live our lives in a way that glorifies God, but when we take on the mind of Christ, we live our lives for Christ in front of others. Even more, your life lived for Christ is for the sake of others. Wow, what an

65

incredible thought. You see, we are bent toward selfishness. You were born with it. I was born with it. We were born into sin, and at the center of sin is selfishness. As we grow in Christ, we begin to recognize the difference between selfishness and selflessness. The picture of selflessness is Christ. His life here on earth was spent serving those who loved Him and those who didn't. This is it. We think that as Christians we should serve other Christians and fight those who are not. Jesus served equally the just and the unjust. Jesus looked for those who were lost and served them explicitly.

Why does knowing this help you? Your life has meaning and purpose in Christ beyond what He does for you personally. God intends to use your life to reach the world for Him.

You have a responsibility to spread the aroma of Christ to everyone you meet.

You must see that other people are your responsibility. Yes, that means the people you like and the people you don't. Think about it. How are people around you going to see God's love for them if you aren't willing to love them? How are people around you going to hear God's voice if you aren't willing to talk to them? How are people around you going to know God's forgiveness if you aren't willing to forgive them? You must move from a relationship with Christ that is about you—a relationship that only meets your needs—to a relationship with Christ that reflects His love and desires to meet the needs of others.

Let's put this all together. Allow the ingredients that God puts in your life to work together to tenderize and flavor your soul. Be patient and allow this marinating process to change you from one who is selfish to one who is selfless. You don't need to fear the fire because you now understand that when you are tested by it, your life will produce an aroma that points people toward God. Now that's an aroma worth having.

THE AROMA OF CHRIST

Discussion Questions

Remember, these questions are designed to help you (and your discipleship group) process what you have just read. It's important to write down your response in the space provided.

1. Who do you know who has the strong aroma of Christ?

2. Do you think other people would answer this question by putting your name in the blank?

3. List five ingredients (disciplines) that you think everyone needs to have in their lives to grow spiritually.

4. How do these five work together?

5. Which of the five don't you like? Why?

6. Are you willing to submit yourself to this marinating process?

7. What do you think this marinating process will cost you?

LOVE
stinks

Why can't we all just get along? Yeah right. From the beginning of the world people have had a hard time just being nice to each other. Your youth group is no different. Admit it, your youth group is full of people who don't know each other, don't trust each other, or simply don't like each other. Recently I did an online survey and asked youth pastors from across the country what percentage of students in their ministries (a) know each other, (b) like each other, (c) don't know, (d) don't like, or (e) don't care. The numbers were shocking. I anticipated a large percentage of responses to be in the "kind of know each other/don't know each other" range. I didn't expect the large percentage of responses in the "don't like/don't care" range. So let's just be honest with each other: There are a lot of people in youth groups who aren't on the friends list.

This isn't anything new, but it is sending a message to our world that says accepting Jesus into your heart does not mean that we will accept you into our group. I'm sorry if that sounds too harsh. I know that not everybody in every group is like this. But almost every gathering of people that has existed on this planet has had problems with this. As hard as you and I have tried to fight this, we have overwhelmingly failed. Every new generation of people needs to learn this lesson, but at what price? What will it take for us to learn how to love each other like Christ loves us?

be nice to everyone

While I was living in San Diego, there were several school shootings that took place in our area in a relatively short time frame. First there was one at Santana High School and then another at Granite Hills High School. Word spread quickly of the shootings, and the entire community, and the entire nation, was shaken. A group of students and their pastor from a church in Littleton,

Colorado (the site of the Columbine school shooting), came to San Diego to minister, to simply care for the students affected. We held a rally at our youth center, Ground Zero, and the students from Colorado were the featured speakers. This tall skinny guy stood up after a time of worship and in front of a packed youth center simply said, "Be nice to everyone." He went on to say, "We need to learn to accept everyone who walks into our youth groups, not just the people we like."

Several other people got up to speak, but the words of that student still ring loud in my ears. Not only do we need to hear what he said, we need to understand why he said it. Why love your enemies? Yes, I know, the Bible says so, but that doesn't mean that we actually do it. In fact, loving your enemies seems impossible compared to the fact that it's difficult to love the people in your own church. If you can't love, or even like, the people who are already in your group, how are you to go way beyond and love your enemies? So here we go. Let's take a look at what it means to love people. Even more, why would God ask us to? I mean, He's supposed to love everyone, and of course He can; He's God. So why you and me? Why is it such a big deal that we care about other people?

We must understand that love is due everyone, which includes you and me. Yes, everyone who has ever been born, regardless of who they are or what they have done, is due God's love. When I say *due*, I mean that God's love is extended to everyone. God makes it clear that we are to join Him in extending His love.

> Jesus replied: "'Love the Lord your God with all your heart and with all your soul and with all your mind.' This is the first and greatest commandment. And the second is like it: 'Love your neighbor as yourself.' All the Law and the Prophets hang on these two commandments." (Matt. 22:37–40)

It's pretty clear: We don't have a choice. Loving others goes hand in hand with loving God. God desires you to have a heart for your world. Learning to care about somebody else is a big deal. We're really good at caring about ourselves, but caring about others seems to be too big a stretch for most of us.

You know what's even crazier? God talks about a deeper level of love that you must have for those who love God like you do. When we finally do connect with someone new and show them the love of God, they come to our church and see that we don't even like each other. What's different about our group compared to the world they're living in? Nothing. We're just like other people at school. We talk about each other behind our backs just as much as those who don't call themselves Christians do. Our message of love, hope, and forgiveness sounds really good in a sermon or a worship song. But clearly our talk doesn't match our walk.

Here's the deal. We may not think like everybody in our group. We may not like the same music, the same food, or have the same kind of styles, but we must have the same heart. What unifies us is not our similar styles, it's our passion for Jesus Christ. What unifies us is not our opinions on worship or if we like our pastor. What unifies us is the fact that our hearts have been changed by the same loving God. For too long we have failed to rally around what we all have in common: a transformed heart. We have allowed opinion, style, and even fear to drive a wedge between people who have the same Father. This very fact has made us ineffective in loving our world.

If we can't come together and love and support each other, how can we expect to be the unified force God desires to use to reach the world?

77

Compassion and love are marks that should distinguish us as people who have been changed by the power of Jesus Christ. Instead we are known for our petty arguments, ugly looks, exclusive meetings, and weird T-shirts. Our lives proclaim a message that is contradictory to the life God desires. God's heart is broken for people who don't know Him; why isn't ours? God's mercy and grace are extended to people who are struggling to know Him as their master and friend; why do we hold our mercy and grace back?

Don't for a second think that we should ever turn our back on sin and ignore it in our community or in our own lives. The foundation of the truth of Christ in Scripture is what we stand on. It is this foundation that frees us to accept the sinner and reject the sin. The joy of salvation that we have in Jesus includes the opportunity for us to walk with others in their pursuit of Him as well. It's what unifies us.

> **For too long we have failed to cling to the one thing that keeps us together: a heart like that of Jesus.**

We have allowed style, talents, locations, and opinion to steal our opportunity to be kind and loving to those we don't know and for some that we do know. The one thing we can all agree on is that our desire is to have a heart that is broken for Jesus.

Let's change the way we see others—those we don't know and those we do. Let's show the people in our world that love and acceptance isn't conditional. The way we treat people shouldn't be based on who they are; it should be based on who God is.

Discussion Questions

Remember, these questions are designed to help you (and your discipleship group) process what you have just read. It's important to write down your response in the space provided.

1. Have you ever felt left out, or even ignored, in your own youth group?

2. Why do you think we ignore people?

3. What can we do to fight our own insecurities and fears of other people and truly reach out to them in love?

4. How can we work together to accomplish this?

81

5. What should be the unifying factor in your church?

6. Are there people in your group you know are being excluded?

7. What are you going to do about this?

83

CAN I do THIS?

✝his is the big question. To ignore it would be a mistake. To allow it to linger unanswered in your head, especially in tough times, would be deadly. The answer to this question is easy—yes! A big fat yes. You can do this if you remain in Christ and He in you. Remember it's not you doing all of the work but rather Christ in you that will enable you to live this committed life that honors Christ, which moves beyond spiritual highs to the true heights of spiritual growth. Again the answer is yes! As you take responsibility for this relationship, hold fast to the truth that Christ desires to do this with you, and He has revealed to you everything He learned from the Father (John 15:15). His knowledge, power, and strength are available to you. You can trust Him even when you can't see Him.

86 Let me say, though, that you will encounter times of doubt. You may doubt if you really know Christ. The feelings you first had with God will come and go. You may even experience times of physical brokenness. All kinds of temptations will show their ugly heads at different points in your life to challenge your relationship and contentment in Christ. When I say yes you can do this, I mean that you can do this on all fronts.

In football they say to keep your head on a swivel so that you don't get blindsided by another player. You have probably seen some of those kinds of hits when you watch football on TV. I love watching football highlights, especially the clips of someone getting blindsided. But I don't want you to make any spiritual highlight clips, getting blindsided by temptation. Stay committed *in* Christ. Stay humble. Stay disciplined and accountable. Simply, stay close to Him.

warning

Even the most experienced athletes can get blindsided. There is no guarantee that you never will. You may not get blindsided by a direct temptation, but you might get hit with a life situation that you didn't expect—parents divorce, an accident leaves you paralyzed, depression, addiction, the loss of a friend. Within that situation temptations will arise. You will question God. You will question your faith. You must know that your life purpose is to glorify God. I want to tell you that you can glorify God in a life filled with blessings or a life full of suffering.

Chad found out that he had cancer his freshman year of high school. To say he was bitter is an understatement. He was scared. He was hurt. He questioned God—and so did I. As his high school years slid by, Chad was hit-and-miss at school. Getting treatment took a lot of time and cost him a lot of energy. There were some really bad days and then times when he felt good. One of the hardest days I had with Chad was driving out to the cemetery together to pick out a spot for him. Chad was the only one who had a good attitude about it that day.

As time passed and Chad declined, we would take students to his house and have a small youth service there after we were done at church. I often wonder who was blessed by those times more, Chad or us. Then I received the call and drove to his house. I still remember

87

the look in his eyes and his final breath. No, it wasn't fair. No, he didn't deserve to suffer like that. Who does? But there was a peace about Chad as he died that night that is not possible without having a relationship with Christ.

So no, I can't guarantee that you will never have to suffer if you commit your life to Christ. Do I hope that you and those you love will never have to go through what Chad did? Yes. But true life is so much more than what we experience during our time on earth. No matter what happens to you, you can choose to glorify God.

fighting your giants

Hearing this story about Chad probably makes what you go through at home or school seem insignificant, but I want to warn you: Don't get blindsided by the giants in your life. Don't turn your head and get blindsided by social pressure; it's a formidable giant to deal with. Don't get blindsided by doubt; it wants to rise up and fight to convince you that what you feel in your heart about Christ and the commitment you made to follow Him are not real. These giants want to deceive you by telling you that what you experienced in Christ was emotional and not a reality you can live the rest of your life. You stand and fight these giants by holding tight to the promise that Christ is in you—and by fulfilling your end of the bargain: You must remain in Him.

You also stand up to these giants by the way you live your life. All of us have a platform, and believe it or not it's bigger than the one at camp or at church. It's bigger than any stage you've ever seen. The stage you have can reach the hearts of people that no speaker, no pastor, and no musician could ever reach.

> You living your life committed to Christ is louder than the biggest sound system ever built.

You living like Christ will say more to your friends, family, and strangers than a book like this ever could.

Do you think you can really do this? Can you keep this commitment you have right now—forever? The answer to these questions lies in your response to this: Does He have your heart? Beyond your commitment or emotionally charged experience, has Jesus penetrated your soul, and have you surrendered every area of your life to His control? If your answer is yes, then you will bear fruit. You will live differently. And best of all you will shine with God's love.

Growing up, I thought that if I would just be a good Christian and do all the right things, then—and only then—God would love me. I was so wrong. I lived my life to get God to love me, and when I failed, my relationship with Him was over. Understand this: You don't serve God so that He will love you; you serve God because He already does. Can you handle that? God loves you even when you don't love Him. God is committed to you even when you are not committed to Him. For me this changes everything. Now I want to serve Him. I want to trust Him. I want to follow Him because I understand He loves me.

So what's next? You've read how this culture wants you to fail. You've learned to anticipate God as He continues to work in your life long after the moment of getting saved. You've separated your emotional ups and downs from your spiritual life. You're smarter than you were before because you understand what it means to be God's friend. You've taken a deep look at who you are and how you treat others. You've asked yourself the question, "Can I do this?"

Now do it. Live as the person God created you to be. Don't allow the giants in your life to stand in your way. Remember that the power, strength, and desire you need are found in Christ. He is the source. When you are found in Him, you will glorify Him and grow. You will follow regardless of where He leads. This thing you feel now is more than a high; it's Christ working in you.

Discussion Questions

Remember, these questions are designed to help you (and your discipleship group) process what you have just read. It's important to write down your response in the space provided.

1. What's your story?

2. What has God done in your life since you became a Christian?

3. What areas of your life are you willing to turn over to God and let Him control?

4. What areas of your life are you reluctant to let God have?

93

5. Are you willing to do what it takes to grow to the next level?

6. What are you going to do today to take the first step?

WHAT NEXT

I. Bible Study

A. Remember that the Word of God is a love letter from God.

B. The Word of God keeps you from sinning (Ps 119:9–11).

C. The Word of God is a weapon against Satan (Heb 4:12, Mt 4:1–11).

D. Ideas for reading the Bible:

1. Get a version of the Bible that your church uses. You will want to invest in a really good Bible that will last you a while.

2. Start reading the Gospels in the New Testament, next read Acts through Revelation and then go to the Old Testament.

3. Get a pen that will not bleed through the page— underline, star, and question mark the verses that you like or need to understand better.

4. Take all the question mark verses to your pastor the next week and ask him what they mean. (You will make his day!)

5. Start little Bible studies at school. (Take your Bible to school.)

6. Try taking your Bible out of your book bag and walking down the hall with it once a week.

7. When you read the Bible pretend like you are in the scene that you are reading and watch closely what is going on.

8. No Bible, no breakfast!

II. Praise

    A. Don't miss this opportunity in your own church—become active in worshipping right where you are.

    B. Tell your story. Just by talking to other people about what God is doing in your life will help you be consistently grateful.

    C. Buy Christian music! Get to know the songs.

III. Prayer

    A. Remember prayer is warfare.

    B. Pray with your own words. Pray real prayers. Pause and engage your mind.

    C. Pray short prayers throughout the day to practice praying without ceasing.

IV. Time Alone with God

    A. Take responsibility for your spiritual health and organize your Bible study, praise, and prayer.

    B. Actually start by marking out one hour this week to be completely alone with God. Then, work this into your life until you are scheduling a day a month just for time with God.

Charlie Alcock is currently an assistant professor and director of youth ministry events at Indiana Wesleyan University. Before joining IWU, Charlie spent 15 years as a youth pastor with the last six at Skyline Church, San Diego, California. At Skyline, Charlie developed a unique ministry called Ground Zero, an off campus youth center designed to meet students right where they live. Charlie's main passion is to see students embrace worship and God's Word, to see them be a witness to their world by living an authentic relationship with Jesus. Charlie and his wife, Joy, have three children, Nathaniel, Nick, and Emily.

To book Charlie at your next event, visit www.KBM.org.